The Dementia Services
Development Centre

 UNIVERSITY OF
STIRLING

Common Problems with the Elderly Confused

SCREAMING & SHOUTING

Graham Stokes
BA, MSc, PhD, ABPsS

Series Editor: Una P Holden

WINSLOW PRESS
Telford Road, Bicester, Oxon OX6 0TS
Telephone: Bicester (0869) 244644

First published in 1986 by
Winslow Press, Telford Road, Bicester, Oxon OX6 0TS
Reprinted 1988
© Graham Stokes, 1988

ISBN 0 86388 043 6

02–151 Printed in Great Britain by Hobbs the Printers, Southampton

CONTENTS

Dr Graham Stokes is a senior clinical psychologist at Walsgrave Hospital, Coventry, with special responsibility for psychology services to the elderly. He graduated from the University of Leeds in 1976 and obtained his doctorate and qualification in clinical psychology at the University of Birmingham. Since qualifying he has worked in the field of adult mental health and now specialises in the psychological management of the confused elderly.

Discovery

1

The Strain of Coping with Confused Shouting

It can be distressing at the best of times caring for elderly confused people as they slowly lose touch with reality and become more dependent upon supporters to look after them; but, if a confused person becomes disruptive and difficult, the ability to show compassion and understanding can seemingly disappear. One of the most debilitating problems carers have to endure is that of often meaningless screaming and shouting.

Whether at home or in an institutional setting, the strain on carers can appear unending as requests for silence are ignored. So why does screaming occur? In part, it is a result of deteriorating memory and declining capacity to think and reason. This not only affects the ability of elderly confused people to explain why they are being noisy, but makes it increasingly likely that they will be unable to recall why they started to scream or shout, or remember that they have been asked to stop. However, repetitive shouting – possibly even singing – is not always closely linked to the severity of memory loss or intellectual deterioration. Even those people who are suffering from mild organic changes and remain reasonably independent may be disruptive and appear immune to efforts to control their irritating habit.

Family Care

Owing to the nature of the problem, it is especially difficult for relatives to manage at home. The typical family does not live in a spacious house with acres of grounds within which they can hide away in peace and allow the confused person to scream or shout until exhausted or satisfied. Being unable to escape from what may feel like unceasing noise can be difficult to tolerate. If your loved one continues to be noisy at night, then the draining effect of broken nights can be an unbearable source of stress. Feelings of helplessness, embarrassment, anger and resentment are commonly felt. Sometimes the excessive strain of managing a person who is noisy can tax resources to the limit and may be responsible for an upsetting breakdown in the ability of a husband or wife, son or daughter to care for their confused loved one at home.

Residential Care

Many residents of ordinary residential homes are handicapped by dementia, and so the strain of caring not only affects relatives struggling to cope with the problem at home, but can also lead to feelings of frustration and despair among care staff. Pleading with a resident who is incessantly shouting or singing aloud to be quiet can fall on seemingly deaf ears. Concern for the well-being of other residents or patients who are being disturbed by the disruptive person may mean that the needs of the confused resident are neglected as steps are taken to protect the interests of the majority. Isolating the noisy resident may seem the only solution. However, this is unlikely to lead to a lasting reduction in the problem and such action unfortunately may also confirm the negative image many people have of institutional care.

When faced with these management difficulties, the need for specialist skills to cope with the problem is essential. The more a carer understands about the reasons for the behaviour the better equipped he or she will be to manage the situation effectively, and the more likely to prevent difficulties arising. Unfortunately, a common impression is that once memory loss occurs there is little that can be done to change the confused person's behaviour. Whilst no 'cure' exists, this pessimistic attitude is unwarranted.

Behaviour *can* be changed and it is the purpose of this book to give practical help to nurses, care staff and relatives on handling some of the exasperating situations which arise when confronting the problem of confused shouting. There are no magic answers, nor foolproof interventions, but there is plenty of evidence to show that considerable improvement is possible.

Keyword Summary

Screaming and Shouting
- A debilitating problem

Family Care
- No escape
- Broken nights
- Feelings of helplessness and anger

Residential Care
- Frustration among care staff
- Considering the other patients

Specialist Skills
- Understanding the problem
- Improvement is possible
- Practical help for nurses, care staff and relatives.

2

Why is it Happening?

In the same way as it is wrong to assume that all old people are alike simply because they are elderly, it is also a mistake to think that all those who are screaming and shouting are doing so for exactly the same reasons and thus will raise identical management problems. There are different reasons why an elderly confused person may start to shout, and each will require a different response from staff or relatives.

Definition

Loud persistent vocalising with no apparent cause for alarm or pain which is resistant to requests for silence. The noisy confused person may scream or indulge in repetitive singing, calling or shouting.

From this definition we see that an elderly confused person who is noisy should not always be regarded as a nuisance to be either ignored or rebuked. While the elderly resident who, for example, constantly shouts for assistance or screams out may risk 'crying wolf too often', it would never be advisable to assume automatically that he or she is doing so without 'real' cause. It is also wise to remember that the elderly confused are unlikely to provide a sensible explanation for their behaviour even if they are alarmed or in pain or discomfort. So always be patient and tolerant when investigating the problem. Impatience may lead to the neglect of the confused residents' needs.

However, once you have identified the existence of a socially disruptive problem, it is important to understand why it is occurring, bearing in mind that the confused themselves are unlikely to know, or be able to recall why they are screaming or shouting.

Possible Explanations

Sensory deprivation

Constant screaming and shouting may be an effort to provide self-stimulation. People need varying levels of stimulation to maintain normal behaviour, yet the life of the elderly confused is often characterised by inactivity, boredom and isolation. Being noisy may overcome an unpleasant lack of stimulation in the environment. Furthermore, creating a disruption in a ward or resident's lounge frequently results in an increase in background noise as others complain and voice their protests. In this way self-stimulation can result in an overall increase in sensory stimulation.

Attention seeking

By creating disruption and noise, a person who is receiving less attention than usual or an amount insufficient for their needs, can force carers to take more notice of them and give them more of their time. As attention from carers also constitutes an increase in stimulation, the elderly person can effectively control their environment to achieve the desired level of sensory input.

Nocturnal disturbance

Confused shouting is often most marked at night. While many elderly people suffer from various forms of insomnia, we should remember that in general old people do not require much more than 5 or 6 hours sleep. Lying awake during the hours of darkness and silence can be an unpleasant source of sensory deprivation especially for those elderly suffering from memory loss. Once again, self-stimulation can be responsible for the onset of apparently meaningless shouting.

Separation-anxiety

As a result of their poor memory for recent information (known as short-term memory loss), a confused person may call out constantly for a loved one whose whereabouts they cannot recall despite constant reminders. This behaviour is especially difficult to manage when the person they are calling for is unobtainable; for example, if they are shouting for a deceased loved one, or if they are living away from their partner in a residential setting.

Stress

Agitated shouting can be an indication that the confused person is upset or distressed. For example, movement to a new placement may result in disorientation and feelings of insecurity. The outcome may be the onset of a seemingly meaningless fear response such as screaming and shouting. Alternatively, the repetitive singing of a familiar song may provide the distressed resident with reassurance and comfort.

Overstimulation

In contrast to the problem of sensory deprivation, a source of frustration-related shouting is that of overstimulation. A confused elderly person sitting in a hectic and noisy room or who is bombarded with repeated instructions may experience an excess of environmental input and resort to agitated shouting. In hospitals and residential settings, such disturbed behaviour often reaches a peak at mealtimes.

So as you can see, screaming and shouting is by no means a straightforward problem either to understand or to manage.

Keyword Summary

Screaming and Shouting
- Several causes
- A definition
- Is there a justifiable reason?

Possible explanations
- Sensory deprivation
- Attention-seeking
- Nocturnal disturbance
- Separation anxiety
- Stress
- Overstimulation

3

Making Matters Worse

Whilst changes in memory and intellect are contributing to the problem of screaming and shouting, when seeking a more complete explanation we must clearly take into account environmental influences and appreciate the extra problems that inadequate living arrangements, poor quality of life and inappropriate management procedures can bring about.

Residential Settings

In some homes for the elderly, inactivity is the norm. Bored residents spend most of the day sitting or lying down doing nothing, with only mealtimes to look forward to. From the time they get up to the moment they return to bed, many people are invariably understimulated.

Having plenty of time to do so little exacerbates feelings of being alone. Despite living with other people, an elderly resident has on average as little as eight minutes conversation each hour. This is usually with other residents, for staff normally spend time with residents only when they are 'doing' something for them. Unfortunately, those residents who are the most confused tend to be even less involved and more likely to be ignored; that is, until they start to become difficult or disruptive. Giving excessive attention to a person who is noisy even if it is borne out of a wish to protect the interests of others, can lead to an increase in the unwanted behaviour, especially if this is the only time they are involved in conversation. Some old people are flattered by attention and will do their utmost to gain it, although others may become distressed or agitated if the approach is one of confrontation and excitement.

Some staff feel that to have a television or radio constantly switched on in a lounge is for the benefit of residents, as they are making available a source of entertainment and information. However, this is a lazy and unthinking way of providing stimulation. If the television is left on hour after hour it will represent nothing more than a meaningless and irritating background noise. This can lead to problems of overstimulation and frustration, and as a result of increasing distress or a wish to secure a means of distraction, the onset of agitated shouting. A similar outcome may arise if residents are made to spend their time in an overcrowded and noisy day room.

Depriving elderly people of cherished possessions which offer both continuity with the past and reassurance can give rise to a feeling of distressing insecurity. Without personal mementos to help someone reminisce about their experiences and achievements, memories of the past fade and seem unreal. Such an unpleasant break with personal history can easily make elderly confused residents feel unsettled and anxious.

Even the physical design of a home and the care regime adopted by staff can aggravate the situation. Unpredictable routines, variable mealtimes, inadequate lighting — especially at night — frequent staff changes, absence of clocks, uniform colour schemes and a lack of information which make it difficult for residents to find their way from one location to another, are just some of the features of residential life which have to be considered when seeking the reasons for disoriented behaviour. It is only a short step from such confusion in a strange environment to the onset of anxiety – and fear-reactions.

Night-time routines can also exacerbate the problem of confused shouting. Often the many hours old people spend in bed at a stretch are for the convenience of staff, not residents. Sticking rigidly to a routine may lead to residents being put to bed at the same time night after night, regardless of whether they are tired or what their pre-sleeping habits had been before they entered the home. The outcome can be restless nights and unwelcome disruption. These difficulties are even more likely to arise when inactivity results in residents cat-napping during the day.

Physical Handicaps

A large number of old people suffer from poor hearing and eyesight, yet these handicaps are often left unattended (as are many minor ailments and illnesses which cause discomfort and irritation), and, unwisely, are not considered relevant when considering why a person may be screaming or shouting. For the elderly who are either deaf or blind, the likelihood of sensory deprivation is even more acute. Living in a permanent world of silence or darkness makes contact with people difficult and involvement in satisfying activity less easy to achieve. If the person with sensory handicaps is ignored they may have to resort to self-stimulating behaviour as the only way to break the monotony of their daily existence.

Trying to Find a Solution

Whilst all these conditions make confused shouting more likely to occur, the reaction to the problem can lead to further difficulties and an accelerated 'deterioration' in the confused person's behaviour. It is often the case that when the disruptive behaviour becomes increasingly difficult to manage, a change in routine or placement takes place. Attendance at a day centre may be arranged, relatives may need a period of rest and so respite care in a hospital or residential home may be requested. Alternatively, a noisy patient may start to disrupt a lounge and be moved to another unit. Whilst the reasons for these actions are understandable, because a failing memory makes it difficult for the elderly confused to adjust to strange and often unhelpful environments, frequent changes serve to increase disorientation, stress and the likelihood of disturbed behaviour.

Unfortunately, the response of some care staff, who may have little knowledge of how to manage socially disruptive behaviours in the confused elderly and are often working under pressure, can do more harm than good. An example is when members of staff employ different ideas at the same time to deal with a problem of confused shouting. This not only causes misunderstanding, but can also increase the elderly resident's confusion. Besides inconsistent work practices, other instances of unhelpful staff decisions include the inappropriate use of medication, which can easily turn a fit, if confused, old person into a drowsy and withdrawn one, and the random removal of the noisy resident from the company of others, which can serve to perpetuate a cycle of under-stimulation and resentment. The unwise use of these methods not only complicates the management problem, but can also obscure the true causes of the disturbed behaviour.

Living at Home

Finally, while it is easy to see how problems can unintentionally arise in a residential setting, when an old person lives at home their circumstances can promote confused shouting to an even greater extent. Spending hours at a time with little to do, possibly alone and feeling neglected or abandoned, can only serve to precipitate disruptive behaviour. If a relative, under strain from the burden of caring, is compelled to respond to their loved one's noisy behaviour in order to try to restore peace and quiet and avoid the embarrassment of disturbing the neighbours, the inevitable increase in attention can result in the unintentional encouragement of the behaviour the carer wishes to stamp out.

Possibly the most unhelpful living arrangement is when the confused person lives alone. Little contact with other people to provide stimulation and a tie with reality may lead the confused person to become so disorientated and under-stimulated that difficult management problems are to be expected. Living in a house that has been familiar for years as the family home is no guarantee that the elderly confused person will not eventually regard it as a strange and alien environment. As their memory progressively fails, agitation and distress can re-place feelings of security and safety and result in stress-related behaviours. Even when a home remains familiar, living alone in a house full of memories can generate unpleasant feelings of separation anxiety, and be responsible for persistent calling for partners and children who may have departed long ago.

Unfortunately, these problems often appear to be the most difficult to resolve. With nobody to keep a constant eye on the confused person and provide information and activity, outside attempts to improve the situation are likely to be unsuccessful. If the disturbed behaviour occurs at night, when community support services are at a minimum, those living nearby may suspect that the needs of the confused person are being neglected.

You can probably think of many other ways in which confused screaming and shouting can be unwittingly encouraged and management made more arduous.

Keyword Summary

Residential settings — environmental influences
- Inactivity = understimulation
- Loneliness = understimulation
- Giving excessive attention to 'disruptive' behaviour
- Unthinking use of television and radio = overstimulation
- Loss of personal possessions and mementos
- Distressing and unhelpful surroundings
- Care regimes and routines
- Special problems at night

Physical handicaps
- Poor hearing and eyesight
- A permanent world of silence and darkness

The response of carers
- A wish to change the placement
- Frequent changes of placement
- Inconsistent work practices — different staff with different ideas
- The inappropriate use of medication — tranquillizers do not solve the problem
- Removal from the company of others

Living at home
- Isolation — little to do and occasionally alone
- Embarrassment of caring
- Living alone
  - few ties with reality and understimulated
  - the difficulty of providing adequate outside support

4

Understanding the Individual Problem

Before tackling the problem of confused shouting, it is important to recognise that while you can describe the reason for the problem in general terms (eg. attention-seeking, under-stimulation, stress), it has ultimately to be seen as an example of disruptive behaviour *unique* to an *individual*. You therefore need to have a thorough understanding of the elderly person's screaming and shouting as it is occurring *now*. Do not rely on guesswork or on an opinion based on a previous episode of shouting.

What is Causing the Behaviour?

Screaming and shouting is not a continuous activity. Even the noisiest resident will not be a constant source of disturbance. In order to understand why confused shouting is not an all-consuming behaviour, taking place at all times, we need to look at the situations in which it occurs. This involves not only identifying when the behaviour takes place, but also noting what the person was doing before starting to scream and shout (or sing) and what the response of carers was to the incident. This task can be easily carried out by following the *ABC analysis of behaviour.*

A = Activating event or situation
B = Behaviour (in this case screaming and shouting)
C = Consequence

Examples of questions which need to be answered under these headings are:

A
- When and where did the shouting start?
- What was the person doing immediately before they started shouting?
- What was happening around them at the time?

B
- What form did the disruption take?
- Was the person agitated, distressed or happy whilst shouting?
- What were they shouting?
- Were they singing?
- How long did the screaming and shouting last?

C
- What was the response of carers to the noisy behaviour?
- Was the person asked why they were shouting; told off; ignored; removed or sedated?
- What was the reaction of other residents?

The ABCs are recorded each time an incident of screaming and shouting occurs. All staff should be aware that the behaviour is being observed. It is best if you record the information at the time of the incident as it is easy to forget the exact circumstances if you leave the recording until later.

As you can see, a Behavioural Analysis provides an accurate and detailed description of actual behaviour in terms of how often it occurred, the circumstances in which it arose and the consequences for the noisy resident. However, to complete the analysis two further areas of information need to be obtained.

Background

First, it is helpful to record the background to the problem. For example, has anything happened during the day (or night) which may have caused upset, annoyance or excitement? Has anything out of the ordinary happened? Is the elderly person on any medication? Has there been a recent change in medication? Have there been recent changes in eating, drinking or toileting habits? Does the resident appear ill or in pain? Does the person suffer from poor hearing or vision? Has there been a recent bereavement? Has the elderly person recently moved to new surroundings?

Life History

Secondly, you must also take into account the elderly confused person's life history. One reason why elderly people continue to shout and sing despite requests not to do so may be because they lead a life of comparative inactivity, following years of interest and occupation. Residents who shout at night may be being denied the bedtime rituals and sleeping habits they observed at home. Those who live alone after years of company may be calling for departed relatives. And conversely, the elderly who previously enjoyed a solitary existence and who start to scream and shout following admission to a residential home, may be finding living with others in a confined space distressing.

The message for professional carers must be 'know your clients'; if you do not know your clients, then the tendency to scream and shout may well be influenced by factors of which you are unaware.

In order to obtain a complete personal history

(eg. previous lifestyle, habits at home and work, patterns of physical exercise, attitudes and expectations, sources of stress, methods of coping with change and stress, illnesses, etc.) not only do care staff and other professionals need to be involved in the process, but so do the family of the confused person.

Recording the Information

The collection of all this information on possible contributory factors can be displayed on a record chart similar to that below (with a covering sheet to provide space for a personal history):

DATE & TIME	A	B	C	BACKGROUND

The Procedure

The first stage in the management of confused screaming and shouting will help identify whether a consistent pattern exists. In order to get a clear picture, the behaviour should be monitored for a period of weeks in order to avoid making decisions on the basis of short-term fluctuations in behaviour. The information obtained should be shared with all carers, discussed during staff meetings and mentioned at 'handover' reports.

Following the period of observation an accurate interpretation is essential because the information gathered during the behavioural analysis decides which method of solving the problem is most appropriate to the person and their situation.

Misinterpreting the Problem

However, before moving on to the stage of intervention, a word of warning. Whilst in most instances confused screaming and shouting is the result of an interaction between the environment and the elderly person's intellectual impairment, in a few cases the behaviour may also be the result of localised brain damage. For example, a condition known as prosopagnosia (i.e. an inability to recognise faces by vision alone), can result in sufferers being unable to recognise their carers even if they should be close relatives. This may result in feelings of separation anxiety and the onset of distressed calling. Focal (i.e. concentrated in one place) lesions in the temporal lobe may result in disruptive outbursts, sometimes unpredictably and sometimes in response to stress. Frontal lobe damage can result in disinhibited behaviour, such as inappropriate shouting, which the person is unable to control. In such patients the emotions appear to run riot.

The existence of such biological changes in the brain are bound to seriously interfere with efforts to manage the problem if they are not taken into consideration. Therefore, assessment of the elderly person by a neuropsychologist should ideally be included in a thorough behavioural analysis, in order to establish the extent of memory loss and whether the presence of other neuropsychological deficits is contributing to the problem. This would avoid the risk of misinterpreting the nature of the disruptive behaviour. However, the expertise to undertake a complete neuropsychological assessment is not readily available, so an alternative option is to be aware of the potential existence of unusual neuropsychological deficits. If close observation of the elderly person's behaviour suggests that it is not related to memory loss but may involve other forms of brain damage (e.g. recognition problems), then request the involvement of a specialist.

Clearly, whilst seeking an explanation can be a lengthy process, taking the trouble to understand a person's behaviour can save valuable time later. Intervening too quickly with inadequate information about the person and their problem may not only be unhelpful, but is likely to result in the problem assuming crisis proportions.

Keyword Summary

Seeking a detailed explanation
- Not a continuous activity
- ABC analysis of behaviour:—
- When and where did the shouting start?
- What was the person doing before they started to scream and shout?
- What form did the disruption take?
- How long did the screaming and shouting last?
- What was the response of carers?
- What was the response of other residents?
- Background information
- Life history — involve the family
- Recording the information
- Finding a pattern — the procedure
- The risk of misinterpretation — the possible existence of focal brain damage
- Neuropsychological assessment
- Saving time in the long run

Management

◇5◇

Stimulation and Activity

The absence of interest, activity and companionship may be responsible for much of the disruptive shouting observed in residential homes and long-stay hospital units. So rather than seeking ways to manage the problem while it is occurring, it may help to increase the amount of stimulation available during the day to prevent it happening in the first place?

Activities

When it comes to providing interesting activities, it is wrong to assume that all elderly residents enjoy 'arts and crafts' or bingo. Find out what their previous work roles and hobbies were and provide similar activities which they are then more likely to enjoy. As a result an activity programme may involve not only traditional activities but small jobs and tasks around the home. Increasing participation in the life of the home means that activity is not a peripheral occupation simply to fill in time, but has a clear purpose for those concerned. You may be surprised how able some elderly confused are when given the opportunity to be active.

For both individuals and groups outings and

shopping expeditions are enjoyable providing they are not arduous and do not involve much travelling. Even though the confused may not appreciate where they are, they will enjoy a change of scenery.

While a confused person who is blind or has difficulty walking is less able to initiate or join in activities, this does not mean they can be ignored. To do so would condemn them to an existence which is starved of stimulation and interest. With patience and forethought activities which can be matched to the elderly person's abilities can always be found. Take advantage of surviving skills, and for those who are deaf or blind, find activities which appeal to other senses, such as touch.

Overall, the provision of interesting things to do is likely to reduce the problem of sensory deprivation and prevent day-time catnapping. Always ensure that the activities provided are age-appropriate, and therefore will not be either a source of strain, nor an insult to their status as aged adults. If an elderly person can only function at a reduced level, in order to achieve a degree of success or mastery, simple tasks will be needed. These may well be similar to those young children enjoy and are able to manage. In such instances never treat the elderly confused in a patronising fashion. Do not talk down to them, nor look upon them as children. Finally, while the provision of activity is to be encouraged, always be careful not to overstimulate the elderly in your care. Take the participants at their own pace, respect their need for rest and appreciate the existence of infirmity which may affect both their stamina and ability to concentrate.

Sociability

In addition to compensating for the loss of activity in the life of a confused resident, feelings of loneliness and rejection need to be dealt with too. If you cannot get family or friends to visit, try arranging for a volunteer helper to visit and 'adopt' the old person.

To encourage friendships between residents try to involve them in regular social activities. Keep group membership constant so that faces become familiar.

It is also important to consider the seating arrangements in the day room or lounge. Social contact between residents is often discouraged by the arrangement of chairs. These are normally situated around the walls, which reduces conversation as most residents find difficulty talking to those across the room or have to strain to turn round to face their neighbour. It is better to place the chairs around coffee-tables as this arrangement encourages conversation. Elderly residents can be notoriously resistant to change, so to help residents accept new seating arrangements provide something for a group to do which requires social proximity (e.g. card games, compiling a scrapbook of nostalgic interest, reminiscence quizzes).

Care staff should not equate talking to residents or patients with wasting time, nor should they feel guilty about doing so. Whilst carers invariably talk to residents as they are doing things for them, the conversation is normally mechanical and often dominated by the task in hand. Not surprisingly, it does little to reduce loneliness. So try not to be too busy to talk with the elderly in your care. Make residents feel they can approach staff readily by always giving a welcoming response. It is also important that care staff make a special effort to sit with those elderly confused who are chairbound because of visual or physical handicaps. A gentle and reassuring touch on the hand or arm can be a pleasant aid to communication.

In many ways it is the responsibility of senior staff to ensure that junior nurses and care assistants understand that spending time with the elderly is an essential part of the job.

Exercise

The scheduling of physical activity will help satisfy the need for exercise. Walks outside in the fresh air are ideal, so if there is a garden available, make full use of it. If you imagine how the senses are bombarded when walking in a garden or spacious ground, it is easy to appreciate how a blind or poorly sighted elderly person in the company of a staff member or relative would benefit from being taken for a walk.

Residents who have structured periods of exercise during the day are more likely to sleep at night. Whilst the exercise should not be strenuous, it is wise to check first whether the old person is fit enough to join in.

Once these stimulation and exercise programmes are introduced, they will need to be a lasting feature of the home. For the benefits which may be gained would not be maintained if the activities were to stop. However, bear in mind that providing the opportunity to become active may not be sufficient. Many institutionalised elderly only too willingly withdraw into themselves and show a general lack of responsiveness to their surroundings. So encouragement from staff is essential. You will need to have both plenty of enthusiasm and ingenuity in order to keep the residents interested and keen to participate in the social and recreational life of the home. If you are successful in encouraging people to participate in the activities provided, supposedly dementing behaviour such as confused shouting can be controlled, and if you are not, then at least residents remain inactive through choice, not as a result of neglect.

Keyword Summary

Interest, activity and companionship

Activity
- Finding activities that are meaningful and enjoyable
- Small jobs around the home
- Outings
- Include those with handicaps
- Take advantage of surviving skills
- Activities need to be age-appropriate
- Never be patronising
- Avoid the problem of over-stimulation

Sociability
- Encouraging visitors
- Social activities
- Seating arrangements in the day room
- Talking to residents/patients is part of the job

Exercise
- Physical activity
- Walks outside
- Visual handicaps need not be a barrier
- Are the elderly fit enough to participate?

Maintaining the social and recreational life of the home

6

Behavioural Methods

Behavioural management has shown itself to be a powerful means of modifying problem behaviour. A decision to use this method arises, for example, when following a behavioural analysis it is decided that changing the consequences (C) of the disruptive behaviour would reduce the frequency of it occurring.

Behaviour Modification

a) A reward system

In general, the basic idea is to deny the elderly confused person fuss and attention whilst they are engaged in stereotyped behaviour such as meaningless calling out. Even angry and critical responses from staff may be counter-productive. They may actually be rewarding, and thereby encourage, further disruption.

However, even if staff manage to consistently ignore episodes of screaming and shouting other residents will respond from time to time and this may serve to maintain the problem. Thus, ignoring unwanted behaviour can only be a partial management strategy. What is also needed is a system of rewarding appropriate behaviour.

When the disruptive resident is sitting quietly or preferably participating in a constructive behaviour, reward them with your time and approval. This not only dissuades attention-seekers from shouting, but improves the quality of their lives by encouraging them to join in the activities of the home. In this way, you are not simply ignoring the problem and hoping it will go away, you are focusing upon building up incompatible behaviours which are both desirable and beneficial.

When giving praise, continue to be aware that you should not treat the elderly person as a child or appear condescending, which may not only serve to annoy but may easily undermine people's confidence and remind them of their failing powers. When communicating with an elderly person, the aim must always be to maintain their self-respect and dignity.

However, this method of control will only work if what is given as a reward is seen by confused residents as rewarding and pleasurable. It is *not* your opinion which is paramount. Whilst the approval and attention of a carer may sometimes be a reward in itself, this is not always enough. In this situation you will have to enrich the life of disruptive residents by providing them with small tangible rewards which they can either use or consume (although always combine such rewards with a social reward such as praise). In the case of a confused blind woman who could be intolerably noisy, physical contact from staff, in the form of rubbing her back, was shown to be successful.

Another option is to provide the opportunity for activity and outings as a reward. Whatever type of reward is chosen, it must be in addition to what is theirs by right, and should not include activities and privileges which are routinely accessible to all.

Another point to bear in mind is to always

consider the relevance of the rewards. If a resident is being rewarded with food, it would not be very effective if he or she had just eaten a meal. Similarly, choosing a reward which is readily available anyway is unlikely to be a potent reinforcer of desired behaviour. It therefore makes sense to have a collection of rewards which can be drawn upon to match the demands of the situation.

If the elderly resident stops making a noise, the reward should be given immediately. Otherwise, if there is a delay they may not remember why they are being rewarded, and so screaming and shouting will continue.

During the initial period of learning, the reward is given whenever the desired behaviour occurs in order that the confused resident develops an understanding of the changed consequences of their behaviour. However, when appropriate behaviour has become well established you cannot suddenly withdraw the rewarding consequences as such action is likely to result in the reappearance of the original problem. This is because sitting quietly or constructive occupation would lose much of its extrinsic appeal, and thus there would be less incentive to continue the new pattern of behaviour. However, you cannot permanently allocate a member of staff to be with a noisy resident. A way round this difficulty is for staff to spend short periods during the day with the resident putting into practice the reward system, and at other times providing the reward when appropriate whenever times allows during the course of the normal daily routine. If maximum opportunity for learning has initially taken place, giving the reward at random times does not mean that genuine behaviour change will not occur. In many ways, being aware that your behaviour will be rewarded, but not knowing when, serves to maintain that response, in this case, silence. This is how gambling can become such a powerful habit! So a policy of intermittent rewarding can serve to maintain the improvement and thereby result in the achievement of permanent change.

To enhance the prospect of successful learning you can make use of a large symbol, such as a red cardboard circle, about 18 inches in diameter. In a training session with the confused resident, associate the presence of this artificial cue with a reward. About four sessions will be required, each lasting about three minutes. When the symbol is used as part of a programme to reduce shouting, the confused person is expecting a reward to be given and this serves to aid attention and concentration as the carer proceeds to give the reward only when he or she is quiet.

b) Learning to discriminate

Through the use of two large symbols of different designs, a noisy resident may learn in which situation shouting or singing is acceptable, and where it is not.

The first design, for example, a green square, would be placed in an area or room (eg. a bedroom) where the disruptive behaviour could be tolerated. It would have to be prominent and colourful so that it could be easily noticed by the confused resident. In the presence of another symbol, say a red star, located in the lounge, quiet room, public areas, etc, screaming and shouting would be discouraged. The elderly person would be led away from these locations with the minimum of fuss and taken to the area or room where in the presence of the 'go' symbol they could continue their habit. In this way the noisy resident would discriminate between symbols and learn where his behaviour would be either unwelcome or allowed to continue.

Information on the reason for the symbols and their consequences can be given in reality orientation sessions. After an initial training period, booster training sessions would be required at regular intervals to make sure the symbols retained meaning for the confused resident. Eventually, the size of the symbols can be gradually reduced as the confused person will learn to discriminate between locations, and will not depend solely on the artificial cues.

c) Punishment

i) **Time out** is a technique in which the appearance of undesirable behaviour is followed by the removal of the elderly person to an unrewarding area.

When confronted with persistent screaming, shouting or singing, a stage is invariably reached when care staff feel the only solution is to remove the disruptive resident for the sake of other residents. This is known as 'time-out'. However, while in theory this should help reduce the problem, in practice such a response from staff is likely to be an inadequate and unwise strategy.

Firstly, this response to the noisy patient is unlikely to be consistently applied throughout the day. Realistically, the confused person will only be removed when staff have time or when the noise become intolerable and is seriously upsetting other residents. Such a haphazard approach would make it difficult for the elderly confused to learn why they are being removed when sometimes they remain undisturbed, and on other occasions they are removed either immediately or following a prolonged period of shouting.

Secondly, the use of time out assumes the person is noisy because they find the consequences rewarding in terms of the reaction they are getting from others, either care staff or residents. Therefore, a logical solution is to move them to another place. As this is a punishment, this is usually one which is isolated and devoid of interest. Removal to their own room may be seen as a reward. Yet, if the person is also shouting for reasons of self-stimulation, removal to an unstimulating environment will simply lead to the maintenance and probable increase in the disturbed behaviour.

Finally, an elderly confused resident will not enjoy being removed to an alternative environment as a result of a time out procedure. So, unless the resident cooperates with your request, enforcing a removal from a lounge or day room may result in aggressive and resistive behaviour. Furthermore, once in the unrewarding environment, the person needs to remain there, albeit for a short period of time. This can create additional problems, eg: how is this to be achieved if the person wishes to leave and return to the lounge? Doors cannot be locked. Such considerations cannot be simply disregarded.

As you see, the use of time-out can generate additional management problems and in the minority of cases, the risk of abuse can be great. Overall, this technique is not recommended.

ii) Response-cost punishment is a procedure in which a person who misbehaves is punished by the loss of a previously available reward.

Having discussed with the confused resident what it is they find enjoyable and rewarding, their daily life is enriched through the provision of this reward on a regular basis, say on the hour or at predetermined times during the day. Select a starting day, and from the moment the day staff come on duty, the resident is able to receive the reward at the appropriate times. However, if the person starts to scream or shout the time of the incident is noted, the resident is informed that the incident has been recorded, and the availability of the reward is withdrawn. To regain the reward the resident must refrain from exhibiting the disruptive behaviour for a set period of time (eg. one hour). If during this 'earning' period he or she displays the target behaviour again, the one-hour penalty recommences from the time of the latest incident (which as before is recorded, and the resident informed). In this way the confused person learns that being noisy means that access to a reward is lost, while following a period of appropriate behaviour a reward is regained. To avoid the patient becoming bored with the reward, establishing a 'menu' of rewards can once again be helpful.

The following case example illustrates the procedure:

Target behaviour	Repetitive singing of meaningless lyrics.
Reward	5-minute discussion with favourite nurse(s) on any topic the patient chooses.

Method	a) Tell the patient that from now on if he does not sing for 15 minutes, each time he achieves this goal you will come and have a chat with him (the 15 minutes does *not* include the period of conversation).
	b) If this goal is achieved go up to him and say "I'm glad to see you have managed to control yourself for a while", and talk to him for 5 minutes.
	c) If the patient sings within the 15-minute period, start timing again and tell him this is what you have done.

iii) Conclusion While response-cost punishment procedures do not create the same problems as time out, as a matter of routine the development of punishment programmes should not be encouraged. On ethical grounds the use of punishment with a handicapped client population is difficult to justify. Rewarding incompatible behaviours is by far the best policy to adopt. If initially these do not exist — although with the problem of confused shouting nobody screams continuously — positive preventive measures such as those detailed in other chapters are required. Remember, prevention is always better than cure.

General Principles

Overall, it is essential that behavioural management operates as far as is possible for 24 hours a day, seven days a week, especially with the more severely confused elderly. All care staff must be involved in order to guarantee that the resident is treated consistently, for consistency is one of the most important features of this approach. The target behaviour, that is the one you are trying to change, must in all cases be accurately defined in advance and be known to all carers.

If behaviour change has occurred within the residential setting or on the hospital ward, it is esential that the improvement transfers to other environments. This is especially so if the problem has been controlled during respite care or at a day centre, and you wish for similar success at home. The technique to use is known as fading. In general terms this involves taking a behaviour that occurs in one situation (e.g. hospital setting) and getting it to occur in a second situation (e.g. home), by gradually changing the first situation into the second.

While behaviours acquired in a restricted environment such as a hospital usually generalise, to some degree, to other settings, there is the risk that putting a person directly into another environment may result in the loss of the new behaviour and result, in this case, in the re-occurrence of disruptive shouting. To facilitate carry-over, it is preferable to gradually fade from the therapeutic setting to similar situations in the real world. This will involve gradually moving away from the pattern of care and activity provided, for example, in the hospital and introducing conditions which approximate those which exist in the home environment. Such a procedure is facilitated by obtaining the co-operation of relatives. If relatives learn the ways care staff have used to manage the problem, they can introduce the techniques of behavioural management at home, thereby giving rise to a similarity across settings which will help support the new pattern of behaviour.

Finally, and possibly most importantly, before you embark upon behavioural management you must be confident that the elderly confused person will be able to benefit from the procedures. While the dementing elderly have difficulty in learning new ways, a degree of learning potential will nearly always exist. Hence, what needs to be done is to match the target being planned for the resident with their remaining intellectual ability. In other words, the goal must be both realistic and attainable. The problem of memory less should not be so severe that the goal will always remain incomprehensible and perplexing. To ensure this does not happen, keep a record of performance and ensure that a regular review of progress by all carers takes place.

The area of behavioural management is one of great complexity even though on a simplistic level it is often understood to be nothing more than a technique to reward good behaviour and punish (or ignore) bad behaviour. It is clearly much more than this naive definition, so if you feel you require an expert opinion before introducing this method of management, seek the help of a clinical psychologist who is skilled in methods of behavioural change.

Keyword Summary

- Behavioural management — changing the consequences of confused shouting.

Behaviour modification

a) A reward system
- When to give attention
- Anger may be counterproductive
- Ignoring problem behaviour — an incomplete strategy
- Reward constructive behaviour
- Building up incompatible behaviours
- Maintain self-respect and dignity
- Find rewards that please
- A policy of enrichment
- Relevance of rewards
- Reward immediately
- Rewards cannot be suddenly withdrawn
- Intermittent rewarding
- Maintaining improved behaviour
- Use of an artificial cue

b) Learning to discriminate
- the use of symbols
- discuss in reality orientation groups
- booster-training sessions
- phasing-out the symbols

c) Punishment

i) Time out
- removing the confused patient to an unrewarding area
- an inadequate and unwise strategy
- haphazard administration
- removal to an unstimulating environment = sensory deprivation
- risk of aggressive and resistive behaviour
- procedure can be abused

ii) Response-cost punishment
- loss of previously available reward
- reward regained following a period of appropriate behaviour
- a 'menu' of rewards

iii) Conclusion
- punishment programmes are not recommended
- reward incompatible behaviours instead
- prevention is better than cure

General principles
- The need for a consistent approach
- Define the target behaviour
- Fading
- Gaining the cooperation of relatives
- Learning potential will nearly always exist
- Set realistic targets
- Record-keeping and regular reviews
- Behavioural management is complex
- If necessary, seek an expert opinion from a clinical psychologist

7

Changing the Environment

Since an elderly person's surroundings can be responsible for stress-related behaviour, such as confused shouting, it makes sense to create an environment which will reduce the risk of this problem arising.

Building Familiarisation

To reduce the prospect of the confused elderly experiencing disorientation and an unpleasant sensation of fear, the use of signs, symbols and directional arrows can be very effective in making the building more familiar. Signs need to be placed in prominent positions and should be large enough to compensate for poor eyesight. Use simple messages — large pictorial signs or symbols are often better than just the written word. Personalise bedroom doors with the resident's name.

In addition to these 'clues', colour coding may also be helpful. By associating colours with different rooms, residents have an alternative key to the geography of the home.

You can imaginatively combine both colour coding and the use of symbols, to produce, for example, the following results:

Room	Door	Directional Arrow	Symbol
Toilet	Blue	Blue	Blue 'T' on a white background
Bathroom	White	White	White 'bath' on a blue background
Dining Room	Yellow	Yellow	Yellow 'knife and fork' on a black background
Coffee Room	Brown	Brown	Brown 'cup and saucer' on a yellow background
Bedroom	Orange	Orange	Orange 'bed' on a black background

There are numerous colour combinations, so you can make your choice blend in with the existing decorations and colour scheme. Always remember to use clear lettering and bright colours.

But it is not enough to simply put up signs and symbols and expect the elderly residents to grasp the meaning. They must be taught to find their way about. You can introduce the information to a small number of residents in a Reality Orientation group. After this presentation in the 'classroom' staff should accompany confused residents around the home a few times. Eventually, residents should be asked what comes next on the route. Also encourage residents to use their own cues. Get them to notice smells and noises which they can associate with the signs and symbols. This will help them build up a lasting mental map of the home.

Do not walk residents briskly from one location to another. Learning should be at their own pace.

The most confused will have the greatest difficulty so teaching must take place regularly in order to increase the chances of learning taking place.

Be patient, speak slowly and use short simple sentences. If residents make mistakes do not get irritated or critical. If they are successful, show pleasure and approval, but do not be patronising. When this period of orientation is over, give regular reminders about the geography of the home in everyday conversation. Although constant repetition may seem boring to you, it is not to the forgetful and confused.

At Night

Darkness can result in the problem of confused shouting become acute. Pioneering work over forty years ago demonstrated that the increase in confusion at night was not the result of fatigue, but was the outcome of sensory deprivation, by showing that such confused behaviour could occur in a darkened room during daytime.

Lying awake at night can result in agitated shouting at a time which is guaranteed to disturb the sleep of others. For this reason, it is easy to appreciate why carers find screaming and shouting especially difficult to tolerate. A solution is to install night lights in the bedroom in order that the environment is gently illuminated, thereby providing a degree of sensory stimulation.

The use of a gentle night light not only helps reduce the problem of self-stimulatory shouting, but it also means that accidents are less likely to happen.

Other changes around the home which can encourage sleep include making sure the bed is comfortable and the room is neither too hot nor too cold, and keeping disruptive routines to a minimum. It may also be helpful to examine whether the policy of the institution is not aggravating the situation by, for example, making residents go to bed when they are not ready for sleep. When interpreting the results of a behavioural analysis carers must always take into account whether the circumstances which are responsible for the problem behaviour are not in turn the result of managerial policy and staff attitudes. Without changes in the latter, attempts to change the former are likely to fail.

Remember the home exists for the benefit of the residents. Routines and policy should be flexible and centred upon the individual's needs. Accordingly, if fear of being in the bedroom appears to be the reason for the elderly person's insomnia, then let them sleep in a comfortable chair elsewhere.

As you can see, changing the environment can help prevent confused shouting occurring. Clearly it is a valuable option for working with the various types of screaming behaviour.

Keyword Summary

Finding the way
- Reduce disorientation
- Signs and directional arrows
- Colour coding
- Learning the geography of a home
- Effective teaching techniques
- Regular reminders

At night
- The benefits of night lights
- Encouraging sleep — restructuring the environment
- The role of managerial policy and staff attitudes
- Individual-centred care

8

Psychological Methods

Specific psychological methods can be used to help ease the management strain of caring for an elderly person who screams and shouts.

Reality Orientation

During times of disorientation and confusion, reality testing is of great importance. Be in possession of accurate information. Remind the person of the time, where he is and who you are. Explain all that is strange and do not take anything for granted. Always correctly identify the person. Whatever form of address is chosen, it should always be used consistently and respectfully.

To reduce stress and anxiety, be friendly, patient and understanding. Reassure the confused that their worries are groundless. However, remember that you also have the task of trying to make people aware of their surroundings. For example:

Time orientation: "Mrs Simpson, it is one o'clock in the morning, see how dark it is?"

Place orientation: "This is Greenpark Lodge, Mrs Jones. This is where you live. See the sign on the wall."

Person orientation: "Mrs Green, my name is Sue.

I work on this ward. Do you want me to call you Elsie or Mrs Green?"

At night, quietly talk to those who cannot sleep and reassure them about their whereabouts. Remind them that it is still night-time. However, you are likely to be at your lowest ebb if you have been awakened by their confused shouting. Despite feeling tired and irritable remember to be tolerant and speak softly and gently.

The most effective way to correct inaccurate and rambling speech is to help the confused realise that their beliefs are mistaken and inappropriate. Be logical and rational. Help them discover the existence or errors by asking *them* to test reality. Do their statements coincide with the evidence? Your approach must always be non-threatening, always ultimately providing the correct information. Remember this is reality orientation, *not* reality confrontation, so do not argue. If the confused resident cannot be persuaded, it is unwise to persist with your efforts.

Finally, the confused with sensory handicaps have an even greater need for reality orientation. If the problems of impaired hearing and poor eyesight cannot be corrected, compensate for the sensory losses by helping the confused identify reality through the use of all five senses: taste, smell, touch, hearing and vision.

Distraction

There is always a need to avoid mishandling an elderly confused person who is already being difficult. As it is not advisable to risk a confrontation, how do you approach an elderly person who is screaming and shouting and encourage them to do otherwise?

An effective method is to distract them. Rather than directly confronting them try talking about something other than what is going on. Approach them calmly and speak in short simple sentences. While respecting the elderly person's need for personal space in order to feel comfortable, placing your hand on their arm can be a comforting gesture. Your aim is to get them to forget their wish to shout and divert them to another activity. If you know your resident well, you should be able to talk about a topic that gains their attention. Talking about the past can effectively occupy the mind of an elderly person. If a resident is calling for somebody from long ago, reminiscing as a means of distraction can be especially effective. It is made easier if the old person has kept personal possessions, such as photographs or mementos, which can be the focus of conversation.

Through giving you guidelines on how to communicate with a perhaps determined and muddled elderly person, these psychological techniques can help you avoid a distressing confrontation.

Keyword Summary

Reality orientation
- Reality testing
- Be friendly, patient and understanding
- Time, place and person orientation
- Be logical and rational
- It is *not* reality confrontation
- Helping those with sensory handicaps

Distraction
- Talk about something else
- A calm approach
- The value of touch
- Reminiscing

The Supporters

9

Helpful Attitudes

Be Positive

Positive staff attitudes are the key to the success of most of the ideas discussed in this book. It does not matter how effective these methods appear in theory, if the attitudes of those who are putting them into practice are unhelpful, they are doomed to fail.

Without being too optimistic, expect improvement. It can occur; deterioration is not inevitable. If success is not achieved with one approach, try another way. Time and time again, the behaviour of the elderly confused improves when thoughtful management is introduced, yet many carers continue to act as if this were impossible.

So, try not to be rigid in your beliefs, and if necessary, readjust your attitudes and expectations.

The Whole Person

Do not simply look upon the resident as a problem to be removed. Instead consider the whole person. Whilst the person may exhibit unwanted behaviour, include this in an appreciation of the person as an individual with a colourful history and a wealth of achievements; a person who has needs, feelings, likes and dislikes.

Even though confusion may be a barrier to communication and thus makes it difficult to appreciate how experiences have shaped an elderly person's life, an interest in the whole individual helps us to better understand the aged resident. This must inevitably lead to an improvement in the quality of care we can provide.

The Problem in Perspective

Do not over-react or feel overwhelmed by having to be responsible for a disruptive resident. Action does not have to be taken. If no harm is being done, ask yourself whether you need to do anything at all. Confused shouting may be unattractive, but is it unacceptable? Sometimes it is best to leave the behaviour alone and accept the situation.

Burn-Out

When many confused elderly are gathered together, problems can appear insurmountable. To manage one difficult resident may be difficult, to care for several can appear impossible. You may approach your work with enthusiasm, yet soon become dismayed and discouraged by the physical demands, unsocial hours and inadequate support.

In these situations you need to share your anger, disappointment and grievances. If you do not, you risk experiencing 'burnout'—feelings of frustration, exhaustion, demoralisation and hopelessness. So, as a regular practice, seek the mutual support of colleagues. Hold group meetings to exchange experiences and concerns. Do not feel embarrassed to acknowledge your doubts and weaknesses, for you will also undoubtedly have assets and strengths your fellow carers may benefit from.

However, if you work in relative isolation and there is little chance of assistance from other carers, try and develop coping attitudes. Dismiss negative and self-defeating ideas. Do not let your mind run riot to an extent where you cannot 'see the wood for the trees'. Be constructive and concentrate on the task at hand. The demands and pressures may appear endless but you will only successfully get on top of them if you tackle one problem at a time. Positive thinking can help prevent undesirable levels of stress and strain.

Overall, adopting the right attitudes can make you a more effective carer, and enable you to help the elderly confused obtain a better quality of life.

Keyword Summary

Attitudes
- Be positive
- Remain confident that improvement will occur

The whole person
- Treat the resident as a person, not simply as a problem
- Take an interest in the whole person — appreciate needs and feelings

The problem in perspective
- Do not over-react
- Is it unacceptable?

Burn-out
- Problems appear insurmountable
- Enthusiasm replaced by dismay
- Burn-out — feelings of exhaustion and frustration
- The need for the support of colleagues
- Coping attitudes — dismiss negative ideas
- Be constructive — tackle one problem at a time

10

Being the 'Therapist'

Not Just a Carer

As we have seen, the effective management of confused shouting is not something which can be switched on and off. It needs to be practised day in, day out. Such a demand for '24-hour therapy' inevitably involves nurses and residential workers.

The routine work of care staff in daily contact and communication with the elderly person means they have a major impact on management. Only those working so closely with the problem can identify the most likely explanations and possible solutions. The more familiar you and your colleagues are with the elderly resident, the more accurate your knowledge will be. Nobody else can possibly be so well informed. No other professional can appreciate the difficulties that arise from day-to-day. In practice, you therefore cease to be simply a carer and become a skilled 'therapist' in your own right.

Medication

Hand-in-hand with an increase in the 'therapeutic' role of carers is the view that the management of disruptive residents or patients does not inevitably require the use of sedating drugs. Do not rely on medication to solve the problem. Whilst sedation may reduce the frequency of screaming and shouting, the possible side- and after-effects mean it should be used very sparingly and be seen as a last resort. For example, the careful administration of prescribed night sedation can encourage sleep. However, if used unwisely it can result in drowsiness and heightened confusion the next day.

Overall, medication is an inadequate substitute for patience, understanding and a regime which satisfies the needs of the elderly confused in care.

Strategy

The guidelines for all therapeutic supporters must be:

1. Identify the reason for screaming and shouting.
2. Make a plan to manage it.
3. Put the plan into action.
4. Evaluate the extent to which the plan is effective.

Such an approach is not only likely to reduce the burden of responsibility but will also improve your own skills and increase the satisfaction you get from your job.

Keyword Summary

More than a carer
- Good management practice cannot be switched on and off
- 24-hour therapy
- Effective management requires accurate information
- Nurses and care-staff are the best informed
- Being a skilled 'therapist'

Medication
- Do not rely on sedating medication
- Possible side- and after-effects
- Drugs — a poor substitute for patience and understanding

Therapeutic strategy
- Find the cause
- Design a treatment plan
- Put plan into operation
- Evaluate the outcome

Managing the Problem at Home

There are around 500,000 confused elderly people in Britain, yet less than a quarter of them are cared for in hospitals or residential homes. This means, without any doubt, that the family is the main provider of care. Typically, the responsibility lies with a partner, daughter or daughter-in-law. Yet relatives struggling to cope with behaviour often as difficult as that found in institutional settings are frequently the forgotten sufferers.

Although nobody outside the situation really knows what it is like to live with a person who screams and shouts, it is hoped that some of the ideas described in this book will make the task of caring easier. To end this practical guide, here are a few more points to help relatives cope with their unenviable situation.

The Future

Confused shouting will not necessarily worsen over time. Nor does it mean that other disruptive behaviours will eventually appear. So you may look to the future with a degree of optimism, for if you are managing your loved one's tendency to shout at present, there is a good chance that this will always be the case.

Coping with Feelings

You are quite likely to have many upsetting feelings if you are caring for someone who is regularly disruptive. Do not be ashamed of these.

If your loved one persistently shouts or sings you can become over-anxious and acutely embarrassed. This can make you feel that you are never free of the problem, so try and place limits on your sense of duty.

It is understandable to grieve for the loss of companionship as major personality changes occur in those you love. You are not alone. Why not seek the company of a local Relative Support Group?

Persistent shouting can be extremely taxing, so anger is a common and natural response. However, try to be angry with the *behaviour* and not the *person*. You may also be angry with fate at having been so unkind and you may be resentful with other members of the family who are not 'pulling their weight'. If you are unable to contain your discontent, you obviously need to do something. Share your feelings and demand support or relief.

Some carers become so enmeshed in their situation that life seems to be a never-ending round of supervision and responsibility. It can help if you try to distance yourself emotionally from your problem. When you feel stressed and anxious, check that your worries are not largely unfounded or exaggerated. Are the neighbours really disturbed by your relative calling out at night? Abandon 'what if . . . .' thoughts. Ask yourself whether there is any evidence to support your fears. Reduce the pressure you feel by avoiding such ideas as "I shouldn't be doing this" or "I must do that". Such thoughts increase the demands you place on yourself and make caring even more tiring. Confused shouting can be bad enough to handle without your inflicting more and more pressure upon yourself.

Some carers benefit from not only placing an emotional distance between themselves and their caring responsibilities, but also, on occasions, a physical distance. Whenever possible, get out, do things, meet people and generally have a break from what may be an upsetting and demanding routine.

Resources

Do not be reluctant to seek professional help. Contact your GP or local Social Services office to request practical support. The Citizens Advice Bureau may have useful tips about local services and facilities. If you want information about the nature of the problem you are dealing with, there are voluntary organisations such as the Alzheimer's Disease Society which are only too willing to provide guidance. Often receiving an explanation can give great relief.

If you are going to provide good care, you must always consider your own needs. Increasing the resources available to you can reduce the cost of caring and ensure that you are able to continue in your supporting role. Encourage other family members to help you share out the responsibility. Do any relatives live close at hand? Could they occasionally come over and keep a watchful eye while you have a day or evening out?

Finally, never feel guilty if you are no longer able to be the sole care giver, or if you are unable to manage without help. These are irrational and self-destructive beliefs. Nobody expects you to be either superhuman or a martyr.

Practical Suggestions

If you are embarrassed by a relative who keeps shouting, visit neighbours and explain the reason for the behaviour. This can only lead to increased tolerance and understanding.

In the home, as in a residential setting, prevention is a better management strategy than trying to think of ways of coping with the problem while it is taking place. So always bear in mind that simple, predictable and familiar routines help reduce the likelihood of confused behaviour.

Work at trying to improve your loved one's memory. This task will be assisted by putting everything in its place and having a place for everything. Make sure there is easy access to everyday information. For example, put up a 'memory board' in the kitchen or any other prominent place. Make sure you include information on the day's activities and especially details of your movements and whereabouts. This is essential if you plan to go out as it will help reduce feelings of separation anxiety. When left alone, always leave your loved one with something to do to occupy their mind.

If your relative wears a watch, make sure it is accurate. If they are fit and able, encourage them to do chores around the house. This will not only give them interest but will reduce their dependence upon you. If confidence can be gained from being involved in the domestic routine, your relative is less likely to feel vulnerable if you need to leave them alone.

Whilst it is advisable to make your absence from home predictable so that it becomes part of a regular pattern, this is sometimes not possible. As an alternative to leaving a note explaining where you are and when you will return, leave a tape recorded (or even a videotaped) message giving factual and reassuring information. This is obviously a more comforting reminder. To overcome the problem of the elderly person forgetting a taped message has been left, intense training will have to take place so they can recall when and how to switch on the machine. Looking to the future, it should not be beyond the ingenuity of the manufacturers of clinical aids to develop a technology by which the recording could play automatically at regular intervals. The equipment could then be made available from GPs or Social Services. Given that so many carers feel trapped by their loved one's handicap, this would be both a worthwhile challenge and development.

Although confused screaming and shouting can make life particularly difficult for supporting relatives, always remain confident that improvement can occur. Use the information in this book to open your mind to ideas and practical suggestions which you may never have considered. It will help you to make the best of what must often seem an impossible situation.

Keyword Summary

The forgotten sufferers
- The family is the main provider of care

The future
- Confused shouting — deterioration is not inevitable
- It does not necessarily lead to other disruptive behaviours
- Be optimistic

Coping
- Do not be ashamed of your feelings
- Over-anxious and embarrassed
- Grief is understandable
- Seek the company of a Relative Support Group
- Anger is a natural reaction — be angry at the behaviour
- Share your feelings
- Emotional distance can be helpful
- Are your worries justified?
- Abandon 'what if' thoughts
- Watch out for the pressure words — I *must*, I *should*, etc.
- Take a break

Resources
- Seek professional help
- Citizens Advice Bureaux may have useful information
- Voluntary organisations
- Recruit family members to help out
- Needing help — do not feel guilty
- You are not superhuman
- Do not be a martyr

Practical suggestions
- Inform neighbours of the problem
- Simple and predictable routines are helpful
- A place for everything, and everything in its place
- Memory board
- Clocks and watches — are they accurate?
- Promote independence
- Going out — provide occupation
  - make absences from home predictable
  - leave a message
  - future technology

—— ◇ ——

Appendix 1

Useful Organisations

Alzheimer's Disease Society, 3rd Floor, Bank Buildings, Fulham Broadway, London SW6 1EP

Age Concern England, Bernard Sunley House, Pitcairn Road, Mitcham, Surrey CR4 3LL

Age Concern Scotland, 33 Castle Street, Edinburgh EH2 3DN

Age Concern Wales, 1 Park Grove, Cardiff CF1 3B

Association of Carers, Medway Homes, Balfour Road, Rochester, Kent MW4 6QU

Coventry Association for the Carers of the Elderly Confused, Newfield Lodge Day Centre, Kingfield Road, Coventry CV1 4DW

Help the Aged, 16-18 St James Walk, London EC1R 0BE

National Council for Carers and their Elderly Dependants, 29 Chilworth Mews, London W2 3RG

—— ◇ ——

Appendix II

Further Reading for Carers

Forgetfulness in Elderly Persons, Advice for Carers, Age Concern.

Coping with Caring — A Guide to Identifying and Supporting an Elderly Person with Dementia, Brian Lodge, MIND, 1981.

24-Hour Approach to the Problem of Confusion in Elderly People, Una Holden et al, Winslow Press, London, 1980.

Our Elders, G.K. Wilcock & J.A. Muir Gray, Oxford University Press, 1981.

Coping with Ageing Parents, C.J. Gilleard & G. Watt, MacDonald Ltd., Loanhead, Midlothian, 1983.

Thinking It Through, U. Holden, Winslow Press, London, 1984.

Caring for the Person with Dementia, Alzheimer's Disease Society, 1984.

Living with Dementia, C.J. Gilleard, Croom Helm Ltd., Beckenham, Kent, 1984.

The 36-Hour Day, N.L. Mace & P.V. Rabins, Hodder & Stoughton, London, 1985.